THE UNITED STATES GOVERNMENT

PRESIDENT

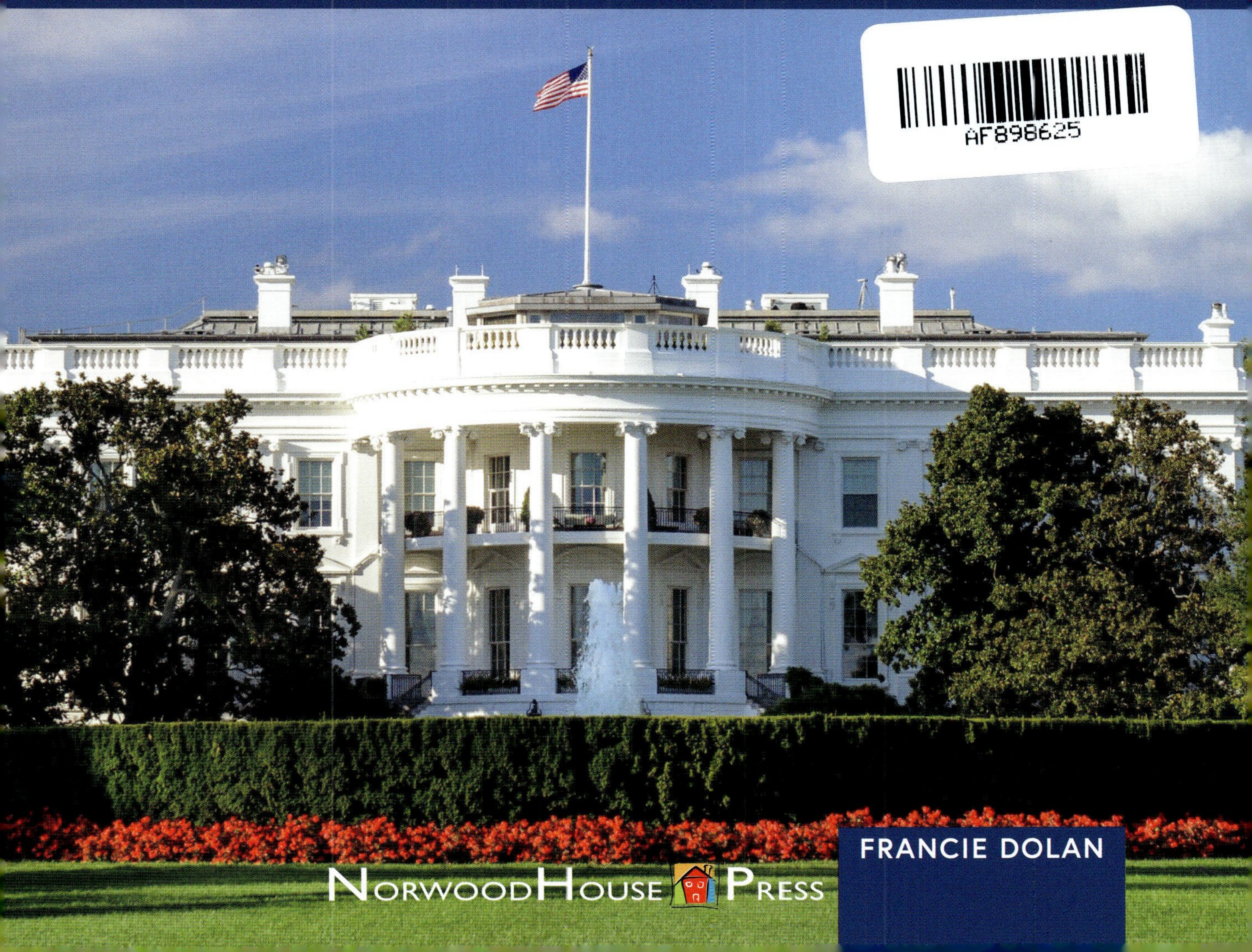

FRANCIE DOLAN

NORWOOD HOUSE PRESS

Cataloging-in-Publication Data

Names: Dolan, Francie.
Title: President / Francie Dolan.
Description: Buffalo, NY : Norwood House Press, 2027. | Series: The United States government | Includes glossary and index.
Identifiers: ISBN 9781978581524 (pbk.) | ISBN 9781978581531 (library bound) | ISBN 9781978581548 (ebook)
Subjects: LCSH: Presidents--United States--Juvenile literature.
Classification: LCC JK517.D65 2027 | DDC 352.230973--dc23

Published in 2027 by
Norwood House Press
2544 Clinton Street
Buffalo, NY 14224

Designer: Rhea Magaro
Editor: Tricia Hoffman

Photo credits: Cover, p. 1 Orhan Cam/Shutterstock.com; cover, p. 1 Sergey Kamshylin/Shutterstock.com; p. 5 VectorMine/Shutterstock.com; pp. 6, 8, 12, 13, 16, 18, 19 Wikipedia; p. 7 Frame Stock Footage/Shutterstock.com; pp. 9, 21 The White House; p. 11 Cpl. Alexandra Earl; p. 14 Castleski/Shutterstock.com; p. 15 txking/Shutterstock.com; pp. 17, 19 Library of Congress;

Printed in the United States of America

TABLE OF CONTENTS

THE UNITED STATES GOVERNMENT

The United States **Constitution** tells how the nation's government is organized. There are three parts, or branches. They are the **executive** branch, legislative branch, and judicial branch.

The president is part of the executive branch.

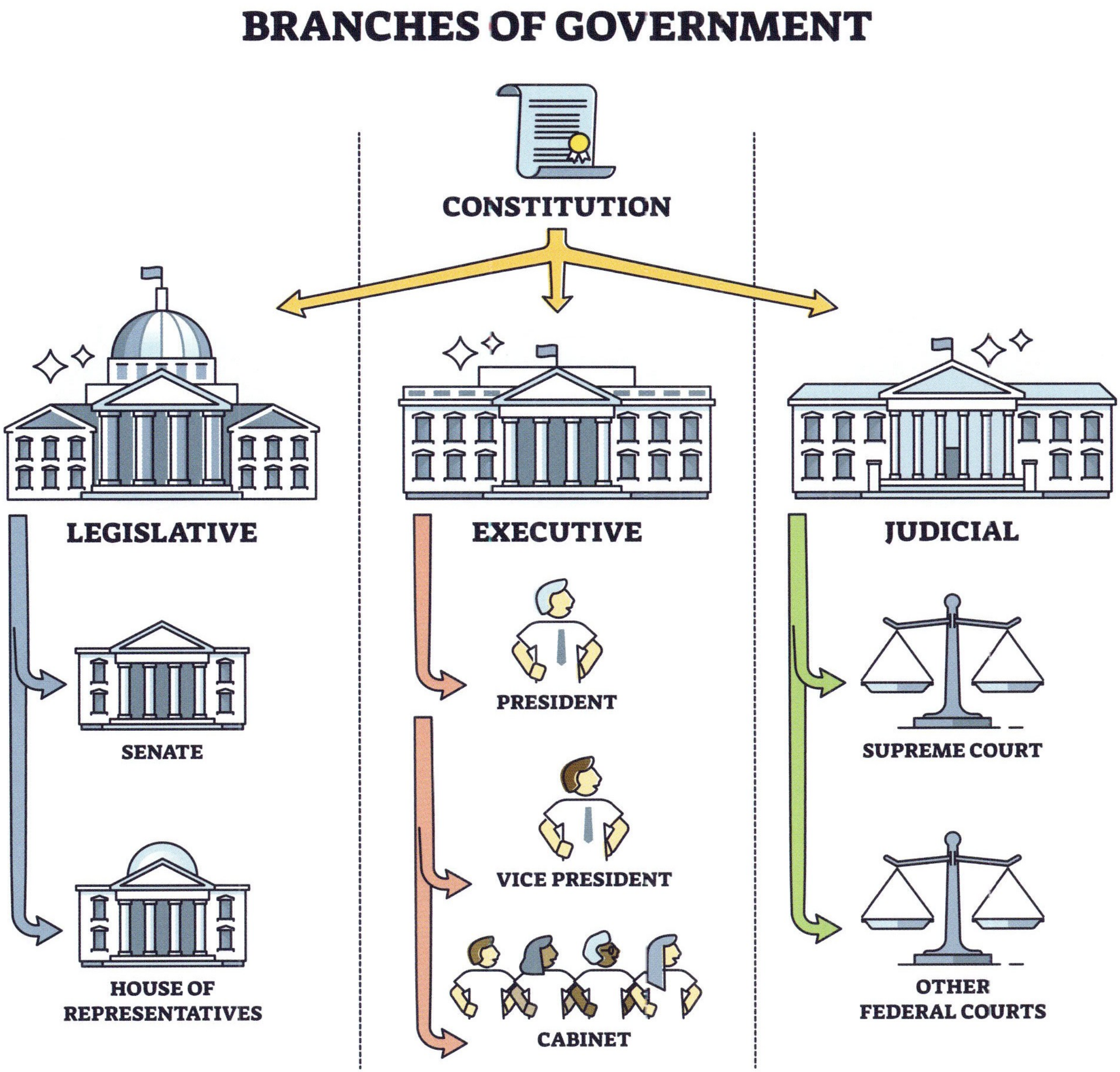
BRANCHES OF GOVERNMENT
CONSTITUTION
LEGISLATIVE
EXECUTIVE
JUDICIAL
SENATE
HOUSE OF REPRESENTATIVES
PRESIDENT
VICE PRESIDENT
CABINET
SUPREME COURT
OTHER FEDERAL COURTS

THE COMMANDER IN CHIEF

Every four years, the American people elect a president. The person who wins gets the majority of votes in the **Electoral College**. He or she moves into the White House.

Electoral College Map

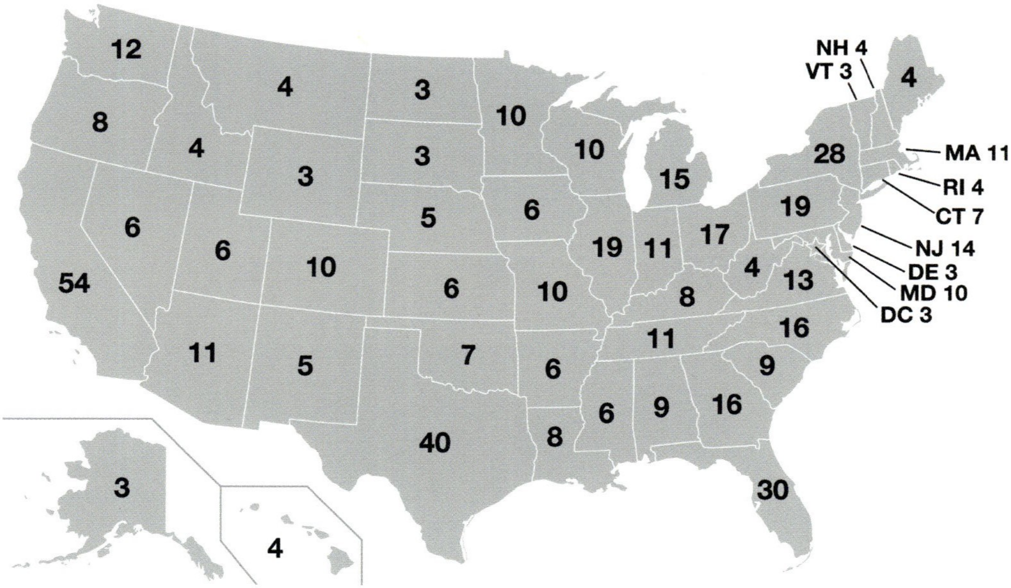

Presidents must be at least 35 years old. They must have been born in the U.S. They must have lived in the U.S. for the past 14 years. They can serve only two **terms**.

The president leads the U.S. government. He or she signs or **vetoes** laws passed by **Congress**. Once laws are passed, it is the president's job to enforce them.

The president chooses **cabinet** members. They advise the president. They lead important parts of the government such as the Department of Homeland Security, Department of Energy, and Department of Agriculture.

The president is the Commander in Chief. He or she is in charge of the U.S. Army, Navy, Air Force, Marine Corps, Space Force, and Coast Guard.

The president makes **treaties** with other countries. He or she chooses **ambassadors** to other countries.

The president also chooses judges, including justices to the U.S. Supreme Court. The president's choices must be approved by the U.S. Senate.

The president has the power to make executive orders. These are special rules that do not require approval by Congress.

The president has the power to **pardon** criminals.

UNITED STATES PRESIDENTS

George Washington was the first U.S. president. The nation's capital, Washington, D.C., is named after him.

Abraham Lincoln was the 16th president. He led the country through the Civil War.

The 26th president was Theodore Roosevelt. He established many national parks and forests.

Franklin Delano Roosevelt, or F.D.R., was the nation's 32nd president. He led the country through the Great Depression.

John Fitzgerald Kennedy, or J.F.K., was the 35th president. He challenged astronauts to go to the moon.

Donald J. Trump was elected to be the 45th and 47th president. He is only the second president to serve non-consecutive terms.

GOVERNING THE UNITED STATES

The president has an important job. He or she is in charge of running the business of the country.

Who is the current U.S. president? How do the president's decisions affect you?

GLOSSARY

ambassadors (am-BAS-uh-durz): people sent by a country to represent it in another country

cabinet (KAB-uh-nit): a group of advisers for the head of a government; cabinet members help the president make decisions and lead parts of the U.S government

Congress (KAHNG-gris): the part of the U.S. government that makes laws and that includes the House of Representatives and the Senate

constitution (kahn-sti-TOO-shuhn): a document that sets forth the basic laws of a country and that outlines the rights of its people and the power of its government

Electoral College (i-lek-TOR-uhl KAH-lij): a body of electors who represent U.S. states and who formally cast votes for the election of the U.S. president and vice president

executive (ig-ZEK-yuh-tiv): related to the part of the U.S. government that carries out laws

pardon (PAHR-duhn): to free from being punished for a crime; to forgive

terms (turmz): definite or set periods of time; American presidents are elected to terms that last four years

treaties (TREE-teez): agreements between two or more countries

vetoes (VEE-tohz): refuses to sign a law that has been passed by Congress; a veto can be overturned by a two-thirds majority vote in Congress

THINKING QUESTIONS

1. Which branch of the U.S. government includes the president?
2. Who can become president?
3. Who makes up the president's cabinet?
4. What does it mean to be Commander in Chief?
5. Who was George Washington?

INDEX

ABOUT THE AUTHOR

Francie Dolan is a writer from Seattle, Washington. She is an American history buff who loves to learn about how her country works and how it has changed over time. She jumps at the chance to travel to Washington, D.C., and visit the capital's important buildings and monuments.